The World's Greatest Composers

Leonard Bernstein

by David Wilkins

OTHER TITLES IN THE SERIES
Johann Sebastian Bach by Charlotte Gray (1-85015-311-6)
Ludwig van Beethoven by Pam Brown (1-85015-302-7)
Frédéric Chopin by Pam Brown (1-85015-310-8)
Claude Debussy by Roderic Dunnett (1-85015-485-6)
Antonin Dvořák by Roderic Dunnett (1-85015-486-4)
Edvard Grieg by Wendy Thompson (1-85015-488-0)
Elton John by John O'Mahony (1-85015-369-8)
John Lennon by Michael White (1-85015-304-3)
Bob Marley by Marsha Bronson (1-85015-312-4)
Wolfgang Amadeus Mozart by Michael White (1-85015-300-0)
Franz Schubert by Barrie Carson-Turner (1-85015-494-5)
Peter Ilyich Tchaikovsky by Michael Pollard (1-85015-303-5)
Antonio Vivaldi by Pam Brown (1-85015-301-9)

Picture Credits
AKG/Berlin: 22, 48; Associated Press Ltd: 41; Austrian Embassy, London: 55; Boston Latin School: 17; Boston Public Library: 13; Colorific: 18/Rob Crandall/Picture Group, 36/Jeff Perkell; Edimedia: 28-29; The Hulton Deutsch Collection: 25, 43(both), 44, 59; Image Select: 12, 33; Images Colour library: 8-9, 10, 40; The Kobal Collection: 39, 47, 50-51; London Features International Ltd: 5, 23, 38/Michael Ochs Archive, 48-49, 52, 60/Michael Ochs Archive; Magnum Photos Limited: cover, 4/Paul Fisco, 26-27, 45/Henri Cartier; © 1995 Felix Nussbaum "The Damned"/AKG: 31; New York Philharmonic Archives: 11, 58; Popperfoto: 9(top), 15, 24, 32, 34, 37, 53, 57(top); Range/Bettmann/UPI: 6-7, 9(bottom), 19, 20, 21, 42, 46/Springer, 57(bottom); Spectrum Colour Library: 35/Viesti; Telegraph Colour Library: 16; © 1957 Times Inc.: 54.

Published in Great Britain in 1995
by Exley Publications Ltd,
16 Chalk Hill, Watford,
Herts WD1 4BN, United Kingdom.

Copyright © Exley Publications, 1995
Copyright © David Wilkins, 1995

A copy of the CIP data is available from the British Library on request.

ISBN 1-85015-487-2

All rights reserved. No part of this publication may be reproduced or transmitted in any form or by any means, electronic or mechanical, including photocopy, recording or any information storage and retrieval system without permission in writing from the Publisher.

Series editor: Samantha Armstrong
Editorial assistants: Helen Lanz and
Alison MacTier
Musical adviser: Jill Simms
Picture editors: Alex Goldberg and James Clift
of Image Select
Typeset by Delta Print, Watford, Herts, U.K.
Printed at Oriental Press, UAE.

Leonard
BERNSTEIN

by David Wilkins

Opposite: Despite his reputation for bringing "show-business hype" to the world of classical music, Bernstein was a deeply serious man. Many photographs catch him in a mood of brooding contemplation. He was a perfectionist – constantly trying to improve on what were already acknowledged to be his great achievements as both a composer and performer.

"West Side Story"

The history of the American musical was changed forever in Washington on August 19, 1957. A celebrity audience was thrilled and astonished by the first performance of *West Side Story*.

Nothing so vital and energetic in its mixture of song and dance, nothing so tragically poignant, had previously been witnessed. The excitement was greatest of all for the show's composer – Leonard Bernstein – who confided in his diary the next morning, "The opening last night was just as we dreamed it. I laughed and cried as though I'd never seen or heard it before!"

When the show transferred to New York for its Broadway première the following month it continued to receive the kind of rave reviews that most composers only dream of. The *New York Times* said, "Everything in *West Side Story* is of a piece. Everything contributes to the total impression of wildness, ecstasy, and anguish." These words, wildness, ecstasy and anguish, could just as easily have been used to describe Bernstein himself, they were the hallmarks of the man the musical world will remember forever.

Genius

Leonard Bernstein's talents were so great and so varied that it may be some time before it is known how and for what he will be best remembered. The largest audience will probably remain for his Broadway musical *West Side Story* and his other

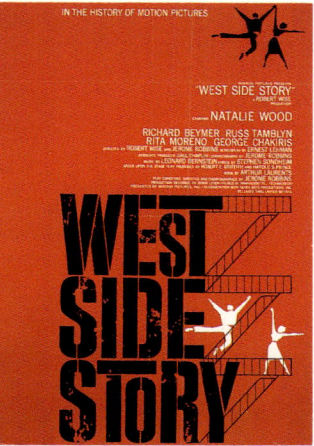

The movie version of West Side Story *won ten Oscars. It won Bernstein an international reputation as a popular composer. It continues to be broadcast regularly on TV throughout the world.*

5

shows, such as *On the Town* and *Candide*. But his contribution to symphonic music will always have a place in American music. His role as a musical educator – his televised children's concerts and university lectures – encouraged generations of concert-goers and record-buyers. As if all of that were not enough for one lifetime, Leonard Bernstein is generally regarded to be one of the greatest ever orchestral conductors.

Bernstein was as happy playing jazz on the piano as he was analyzing a Mozart symphony, conducting an opera in Vienna or Milan, enthusing a school choir, or rubbing shoulders with the stars of Hollywood. He did not believe that music could be "high or low brow" – he thought that it was the greatest joy in life.

Bernstein lived his life with all the energy and flamboyance that he brought to his music making.

Leonard Bernstein became one of the most successful orchestral conductors in the world. He conducted a vast range of music from the time of Vivaldi and Bach through to the major composers of his own century. When conducting he identified so closely with the music that he often felt that he had composed it himself. Depending on what he felt the music expressed, he might seem to be in a deep trance or a frenzy of energy.

He loved to be involved in social and political causes throughout the world. He would invariably travel with a large group of assistants to look after his every need, like a member of a royal family. He was a showman and he would not be ignored.

Some people hated him for this showmanship, but the majority admired and loved him. One player in the New York Philharmonic Orchestra said, "He can come out and conduct in pink tights for all I'm concerned!" They knew that he simply could not be any different. His talent and personality were what made him Leonard Bernstein.

Magical spirit

It is impossible to imagine Leonard Bernstein coming from anywhere other than the United States. The country combines crowds and confusion, vastness,

"That Bernstein was a paramount musician is, of course, beyond question. Composer of the ultimate Broadway musical, aerodynamic concert conductor, bringer of music into millions of homes with his . . . telelectures. A compact, complex charisma, bristling with nervous energy, he could not enter a crowded room without everyone within it feeling somehow touched by him, and elevated."

Norman Lebrecht,
from The Daily Telegraph, 1994.

The Statue of Liberty in New York was a physical symbol of the freedom and opportunity that so many immigrants hoped to find in the United States. It was a gift from the people of France who felt that the American Constitution had much in common with their own pursuit of "Liberty, Fraternity and Equality." Its three-hundred-foot (92m) high construction of 225 tons (221 tonnes) of copper sheeting was shipped from France to New York in 1885. It was erected near the major immigration station of Ellis Island to give a cheering first impression for arrivals in the New World.

and a pioneering spirit into a cocktail of energy. An appreciation of this magical spirit is vital to an understanding of the success of Leonard Bernstein.

In fact, Bernstein was only first-generation American. Both his parents were born in Russia – living surprisingly close to each other in what is now named Ukraine – but it needed the United States to bring them together.

For a mass of people, particularly from Eastern Europe and Russia, the United States acted like a magnet with its emphasis on democracy and opportunity. This was especially so for those who suffered periodic attacks and persecution in their own country. Anyone whose home life was a mixture of poverty, toil, and discrimination looked to the United States as the golden land where ambition would triumph, where anything was possible.

Land of opportunity

Few, if any, types of immigrant were as anxious to reach the shores of the United States as members of the Jewish faith. The persecution that they suffered during World War II was a great incentive to flee to a new country and the chances offered by the United States easily sealed their choice of destination. Leonard's father, Sam Bernstein, arrived in the United States in 1908 to join his uncle who had already made the journey searching for the road that was paved with gold.

Such was the dream! The reality was that, while the dream could certainly come true, it had to be worked for. Sam had the drive that was so important to "making-it" in the new country and was willing to work – first in a smelly fish market in New York and then in his uncle's barbershop in Connecticut. From there he moved to a company that supplied hairdressing and beauty products and he became based in Boston.

Leonard's mother, Jennie Resnick, worked in the textile industry about an hour's drive from Boston. When she met Sam, the pair found that they had so much to talk about – the coincidental proximity of their birthplaces, now so many thousands of miles away, and the profound respect for their Jewishness which mattered more to them than anything else.

Sam and Jennie married in October 1917 and their first child, initially named Louis at Jennie's parents'

Above: Leonard's father, Sam, worked hard to progress from the waterfront fish market of his first job to become a successful businessman.
Below: Despite early disagreements over his future, Leonard remained devoted to his parents, and their pride in his achievement was a major source of happiness for him.

"He had grown up on popular songs on the radio and the traditional music of the synagogue, conflicting influences that were always there when he came to compose, even in <u>Candide</u> and <u>West Side Story</u>."

John Wells,
from The Daily Telegraph, 1994.

All boys of the Jewish faith are received into the adult community at the age of thirteen. This ceremony of initiation is called Bar Mitzvah. The boy learns how to read a passage from the Jewish Bible – the Torah – in Hebrew. The religious ceremony is usually followed by a proud family gathering where the newly "grown-up" boy makes a little speech before the party begins. Leonard, who seems never to have known a moment of shyness or inhibition, loved the whole thing. He made a speech in English and Hebrew and, as a reward, his father presented him with a new "baby grand" piano.

request, was born on August 25, 1918 in Lawrence, Massachusetts. Louis became Leonard, a name preferred by Jennie and Sam, and, although his parents would not know it for many years, the making of Leonard Bernstein had begun.

"How's Lenny?"

The Bernstein's marriage was never a very successful match. Sam saw himself as a scholar of the Jewish religion and spent as much time as possible immersed in the book of Jewish teaching, the Talmud. He wanted his son to be a priest of the faith, a rabbi. Jennie's maternal instincts, on the other hand, were more liberal and she wanted her son to choose his own path in life. This conflict between his parents came to a climax when Leonard began to show an interest in music.

In the meantime, however, there were more urgent issues to consider, such as Leonard's health. Leonard was a sickly child and suffered from serious asthma

10

attacks. His breathing problems caused a number of emergencies in his infancy and his father's first words on returning from a day's work were often, "How's Lenny?"

"To my first love, the keyboard"

Leonard was ten when he met his "first love," the piano, and it was more or less by accident. His father's sister, Aunt Clara, had come to live in the United States and she owned a piano. When Aunt Clara's fourth marriage failed she had a nervous breakdown and was placed in a mental asylum. Leonard's father made himself responsible for her property and moved the piano into his own house. It took Leonard no time at all to decide that the new "toy" was going to be his best friend. "I remember touching this thing the day it arrived, just stroking it and going mad," he said. "I knew from that moment to this, that music was 'it.' There was no question in my mind that my life was to be about music."

Sam didn't approve of his son's pursuit of a musical future because it went against his desire to see his son become a rabbi and because his only

Lenny became a very accomplished pianist, but he never achieved the technical skill of a true virtuoso. His concerto performances as both pianist and conductor was exciting and innovative but his repertoire of pieces was small. He specialized in the concertos of Ravel, Shostakovitch, and one or two by Mozart and Beethoven. His most loved piece was probably Gershwin's Rhapsody in Blue. *It is unlikely that he could ever have made a career as a solo pianist alone, but his ability to put over his ideas on the piano was a great boost to his success as a musical educator.*

Mozart was one of a relatively small number of musicians who achieved incredible technical facility on an instrument while still very young. Bernstein started later and was never equal to such a genius in this way, but he used his ability on the piano to explore a massive range of music and to get to know from the inside the music that he loved to perform.

"The only way one can really say anything about music is to write music."

Leonard Berstein, from The Joy of Music.

experience of professional musicians was the gypsy fiddlers he had known in Ukraine. He wanted a son he could be proud of and, for the moment, he could not see that encouraging Leonard in his piano lessons held any prospect for success or glory. He actively set himself against his son's musical advancement, wanting him to join what was now the growing family business of beauty supplies. Fortunately, his wife knew their son rather better.

Aunt Clara's piano

Leonard was not a prodigy, or child genius, in quite the same way as Mozart who was writing orchestral compositions at the age of eight. It was soon obvious, however, that Leonard shared an essential skill with illustrious musicians – he possessed an incredibly fine "ear" for music.

It is uncommon to find musicians who, when asked to play a piece they do not know, are able to say, "You sing it and I'll play it." To find this ability in a young person who has no musical training or experience is rare. Leonard was able to "pick-out" tunes he heard on the radio on Aunt Clara's piano after only a few weeks.

The boy was so captivated by the sounds he could produce that he demanded piano lessons. His mother's insistence overcame his father's doubts, and before long Leonard's first teacher was employed. The student soon outgrew the teacher and needed increasingly qualified and experienced instruction. He learned to read music very quickly and, by eleven, knew the basics of melody and harmony and was playing Chopin and Bach. Within eighteen months of Aunt Clara's piano arriving, Sam had bought his son a decent grand piano and Leonard was enrolled as a student at the New England Conservatory of Music.

Play as you learn

During this period Leonard began to develop a fondness for many different styles of music. The word "eclectic" – choosing and combining from many different sources – would often be used to describe his compositions in later years.

At the piano, he was taught all the necessary technical skills: "It came to me like drinking water," he said. He was also introduced to the classical repertoire of Bach, Mozart, and Beethoven. He loved to play popular songs, as well, to delight and impress his family. "I loved all music," Leonard recalled, "and I loved to dance."

Sam Bernstein was still not accustomed to the idea of his son devoting himself to music, but his attitude became less aggressive. Leonard was showing that his dedication was total and his teachers considered his talent to be unquestionable.

The New England Conservatory of Music was the obvious place for Leonard to expand his musical knowledge. It was here that he gained much of the essential groundwork in a variety of musical techniques and styles.

> *"We couldn't know that he was going to be the conductor he turned out to be, but it was clear he was an exciting, talented musician who would have some kind of a dazzling career ahead of him. There was no doubt about that. He was a kind of magnetic force."*
>
> *James Chambers, Bernstein's old friend and horn player in the N.Y. Philharmonic Orchestra.*

A teacher and a friend for life

Boston's most famous piano teacher was Heinrich Gebhard. Leonard soon saved the $25 necessary for an audition with him by playing in a jazz band for as many sessions as possible. Gebhard was impressed by the boy's musical ability, but suggested that his assistant would be a better first teacher for him. Her lessons would be cheaper and she could bring his piano technique up to the standard that Gebhard required of his pupils.

So Leonard came into contact with Helen Coates who was to remain an indispensable part of his life for over fifty years. It was Miss Coates, as she preferred to be called, who first recognized the true extent of Leonard's talents. She worked with him on exercises and pieces that would help to perfect his playing, but she was also vital in encouraging his general education. Miss Coates advised him to borrow music scores from the library and get to know as much music as possible; she also insisted that he develop his awareness of literature, languages, and general knowledge.

Discipline and comfort

She introduced him to "new" music. They would sit together and listen to music broadcasts of composers such as Prokofiev, also an influential pianist, and Stravinsky. Before that time, Leonard had thought of "serious" music as something with only a past – music that had already been written. From Miss Coates' guidance he learned not only that it had a very active present life, but also a future, and he determined to be part of it.

"As a teacher she introduced me to discipline, to the most profound meaning of work, to the control and penetration of musical beauty," Leonard remembered. "She also listened to my problems, musical and non-musical, gave liberal and sage counsel and comfort." In fact, Miss Coates was the first of a few revered characters without whom Leonard Bernstein could not have developed into the genius he became.

The music of Igor Stravinsky, pictured right, had a profound influence on Bernstein. Like Bernstein himself, he composed in a variety of styles without ever losing his own "voice." Bernstein was a constant champion of Stravinsky's music and his recordings of many of the composer's major works are still considered to be among the best available. The Canadian Glenn Gould, in the middle, one of the great eccentric and mysterious pianists of the century, whose performance of a concerto by Brahms Lenny felt obliged to explain to the audience just before he conducted it!

American music and all that jazz

Bernstein wasted no time in his exploration of the musical scene that surrounded him. Before the twentieth century, the works of American composers were largely copies of what was being written in Europe – without any distinctive "sound" to make them immediately identifiable as American.

The massive immigration to the United States brought a richness of musical heritage. This provided the wealth of different influences that Bernstein came to love and to use in his own composing. The songs and psalms of the English came with the Puritan settlers, the Lutheran chorales familiar from the time of Bach came from the Germans and the music of the French, Swedish, and Eastern European communities all added something to the musical world of the developing country. Most important of all were the rhythms of the African Americans that form the basis of jazz.

Jazz, it has been said, is a very loose term to describe a wide variety of compositions, and its history provides a fascinating study of its own. The qualities that can be most easily associated with it are to do with rhythm – the feeling of strong and weak beats or pulses in the music, and melody – the shape of the tune. Jazz relies on syncopation – where

Jazz was initially the music of the black population of the United States and had a greater impact on American music in the twentieth century than any other influence. The African American people, who were denied their liberty in so many social and political respects, used the freedom of jazz forms to express both the anguish of their situation and their sense of fun.

the strong beats do not always come where they are expected, and on blues notes – where some of the sounds in the melody are different from those found in the usual patterns of western music. "I love it because it is an original kind of emotional expression in that it is never wholly sad or wholly happy.... I love it also for its humor. It really plays with notes.... It 'fools around' and has fun with them....," Bernstein said of jazz. Probably the most famous composer having fun in this way while Bernstein was growing up was George Gershwin.

From schoolboy to student

Although his musical studies were central to him, Leonard Bernstein also attended the most prestigious school in the area, the Boston Latin School. He proved to be a diligent student and excelled in all subjects and won numerous academic awards. Unfortunately, he also started his lifetime smoking habit.

During the long summers, the fourteen year old arranged performances of the operettas of Gilbert and Sullivan with family and friends. These took place at a leafy, lakeside town outside Boston, where the increasingly wealthy Bernstein family had a summer-house. His father's suspicions about the pursuit of a musical career had not entirely disappeared, but he was happy enough to arrange Leonard's first broadcast performance – part of a fifteen-minute broadcast on a small radio station advertising Sam Bernstein's beauty products!

Turning point

In May 1932 Sam arranged a musical outing with his son. This was to prove to be another turning-point in sealing the young Bernstein's ambitions. Together father and son attended a symphony orchestra concert, the first for both of them, given by the Boston Pops Orchestra.

Among the works played was Ravel's *Bolero* – a piece that was beginning to capture the imagination of concert-goers all over the world with its hypnotic repetition of Spanish rhythms. Leonard was overwhelmed by the experience, and his fascination with the man who stood before the orchestra, conjuring those wonderful sounds merely by the waving of his arms, sowed another significant seed of interest in his mind.

The Boston Latin School was renowned for its educational excellence and it was a matter of great pride to the Bernstein family that Leonard was able to gain a place there. He pursued his musical interests outside the school, but it was of tremendous importance to his general education. It was here that he began to devote himself to a cultural education and, especially, foreign languages. Later, the ability to speak to orchestras in French, German, and Italian was a significant aid to his career.

Next stage

After Leonard Bernstein left the Boston Latin School at seventeen he survived one miserable month working for his father's business. It was obvious to them both that this arrangement would never succeed. Leonard's mother gave her son complete support and, with the help of Helen Coates and backed by the boy's remarkable school record, Sam was persuaded that Leonard should apply for a place at Harvard University.

Sam grumbled at the choice of music as a subject for serious study, but when his son was accepted at this most famous of American universities he was happy to exchange opposition for the warm glow of a father's pride.

Big personality

Leonard Bernstein's time at Harvard University was not a completely happy one, but it did give him an essential university opportunity to extend his musical knowledge. More importantly, it also gave him the chance to meet some of the people who would help to advance his career and remain significant friends and mentors for years to come.

Harvard University is the oldest and one of the most respected educational institutions in the United States. It was founded in 1636 in New Towne – later called Cambridge because of its English-style ambitions – and named after John Harvard, who left half his estate and his library to the university. For Bernstein, it was a place of mixed feelings. He was able to greatly expand his theoretical knowledge, but found limited opportunities for practical music-making.

One of the major problems that he encountered for the first time was anti-Semitism. From the beginning, Harvard had been the automatic home of "WASPs" – White Anglo-Saxon Protestants from rich backgrounds – and Jewish students from immigrant families were often looked down on and regarded as second-class citizens.

Leonard was a handsome young man and full of energetic fun. He was a popular character and always had a lot of friends. His natural charm and undoubted talents did much to overcome the resistance, but he was left with a lingering sense of being something of an outsider. This feeling may have caused him to overcompensate by becoming a bit of a show-off and attention seeker – an accusation that he was forced to hear many times in his life.

Still not right

Another great problem with his study at Harvard was that it concentrated on the theory of music, rather than providing opportunities for playing and performing. He said later that, "You could spend hours wandering through the Music Building and never hear a note of actual music."

This emphasis on the "blackboard" side of music

During his time at Harvard, Leonard began to play with the idea of becoming a conductor. As with all university music departments, the students were anxious to perform as much as they could. It was at this time that Bernstein became involved in arranging productions of the operettas of Gilbert and Sullivan – an influence that would be very important to him when he began to compose his own operetta, Candide.

The Greek Dimitri Mitropoulos was the first conductor whom Bernstein came to idolize. His flamboyant bodily gestures were to set the pattern for Bernstein's own style. Mitropoulos' almost religious attitude to the art of conducting kept him going even when his health was threatened. In 1960 he died while conducting a rehearsal of Mahler's 3rd Symphony at La Scala in Milan.

was totally opposite to Bernstein's desire to use music for communication. Later, he was grateful for his grounding in analyzing various musical forms, but at the time he felt that his natural desire to make music was being frustrated.

The good times of university life were fun. Leonard played for the college film society – improvising music for silent films, arranging concerts with small groups of friends, or beginning to explore the delights of conducting. He was also the music critic for the college newspaper.

Of more lasting importance were Leonard's first meetings with three very different characters who each influenced one of the paths – conducting, composing, both serious and light, and performing – all of which would map the course of Leonard Bernstein's future.

A Greek bearing gifts

In January 1937, the Boston Symphony Orchestra engaged the Greek conductor Dimitri Mitropoulos for a number of concerts. One of these coincided with a visit to Harvard by Leonard's mother, Jennie. Leonard had heard that there was to be a party for the conductor and, though he had not been invited, he decided that he would take his mother along and they would both meet the great man. Jennie was against the idea, not least because she felt inadequately dressed for such an occasion, but Lenny would not be dissuaded.

Mitropoulos was quickly charmed by the nineteen year old's wit and his confident personality and asked him to entertain the guests by playing the piano. Bernstein, who never enjoyed a party unless he was able to play the piano, was happy to oblige with some Chopin and a piece of his own. Mitropoulos later said that the experience of encountering Bernstein's talent was like a religious revelation. He was completely captivated.

As a result, Mitropoulos invited Bernstein to

Bernstein succeeded Mitropoulos as musical director of the New York Philharmonic Orchestra. Their relationship was intellectually satisfying for both men, but there were always suggestions that Mitropoulos, as a homosexual, had a more personal reason for supporting Leonard's career.

attend his next orchestral rehearsal and promised to do all he could to aid the young man's career which he decided, without any further evidence, should be as a conductor.

Mitropoulos was a homosexual and it has been said that he found Bernstein physically attractive. For his part, Bernstein had girlfriends, but he also knew that he was attracted to members of his own sex. Whatever the balance of his motives, Mitropoulos was the first to fire Bernstein's ambitions in the direction of conducting and went on to provide much practical help and guidance in the years to come.

"My Broadway buddy"

In the summer of that vital year of 1937, Leonard had a job as a counsellor at a youth camp in northern Massachusetts where he was responsible for teaching

"Bernstein's chutzpah, charisma and high-voltage personality, stemmed from a hunger for life and an almost naive curiosity."
June Ducas,
from the Sunday Express, 1994.

21

American composer, pianist, and conductor George Gershwin, was a great influence in the development of Bernstein's music and career. Gershwin incorporated the spirit of jazz into many of his compositions for Broadway, movies, and the concert stage. His style is often apparent in many of Bernstein's own works.

music and swimming. He loved working with children and his skills as a communicator were already well enough developed to ensure that he got the best out of the young people in his charge.

Sunday July 11 fell on parents' weekend at the camp and Leonard had been asked to play the piano during lunch. At first he refused because he didn't like the idea of playing against the background of crashing cutlery and noisy eating. But that morning he awoke to the news on the radio that George Gershwin had died aged thirty-eight. Lenny was horrified at the loss of one of his idols and changed his mind about playing the piano. During lunch he called for silence, announced the sad news and gave a memorial performance of one of Gershwin's piano preludes. He asked that no applause be given. Everybody present was deeply moved. "As I walked off I felt I *was* Gershwin," he said referring to how he identified with the composer.

A much happier event that summer was his first meeting with the man who became his "Broadway buddy" and the writer of lyrics for his musicals. Bernstein arranged a performance of the Gilbert and

Sullivan operetta *The Pirates of Penzance*. Playing the Pirate King was a young man with an incredible gift for words, Adolph Green. The two men became great friends and went on to share spectacular musical successes as well as a devotion to having "fun," as Leonard liked to say.

Leonard always thought of Adolph Green as his "Broadway buddy." Their friendship went far beyond that of composer and writer and into the realms of great musical partnership. More important than anything else, they shared a tremendous sense of fun. There can be no doubt that without Adolph Green, Bernstein's career as a composer of popular Broadway musicals would never have achieved the success that it did.

Mentor

Although Bernstein always loved to play the piano at parties, he didn't always please his fellow guests with what he chose to play. He had a phenomenal memory for all kinds of music and was happy playing classical music, jazz or hits from the latest Broadway shows, but he also had a fondness for difficult pieces by modern composers that were not immediately attractive. One such piece was the *Piano Variations* by a Jewish-American composer, eighteen years older than himself, Aaron Copland.

Like Bernstein's, Copland's parents had emigrated to the United States from different parts of Russia and, also like his own, the Copland family were devout in their Jewish faith. Copland, too, had met parental resistance in pursuing his wish to become a musician, but he had studied in New York and Paris and was greatly influenced by the music of Stravinsky. When he returned to the United States he incorporated jazz elements into his music.

"Mr. Bernstein writes with zest and with a great deal of relish for the contrasts possible in his instrumental combination. The piano part is especially interesting in its lively rhythms and colorful harmonic effects. Mr. Bernstein is clearly influenced by the generation of American composers that include Copland and Schuman."

Howard Taubman, from the New York Times.

Aaron Copland was the person that Bernstein acknowledged to come the closest to being his composition teacher. Their mutual Jewishness and homosexuality made the two men close friends. Copland is considered by many to have brought a particularly American sound to the symphonic music that was inherited from European models.

In many ways, both personally and musically, Aaron Copland is considered to be the composer who had the greatest influence on Bernstein's own style. It has been said that without Copland, Bernstein would not have existed as the serious composer of symphonic music within the great American tradition.

Modern influences

Bernstein fell in love with Copland's music as soon as he discovered it. He became so obsessed with the *Piano Variations* that he played it at every opportunity, including at parties. "I could empty a room, guaranteed, in two minutes," Bernstein would say with some pride!

Also in 1937, Bernstein and a college friend went to New York for a ballet performance at the Guild Theater. Such an outing was rare because of the shortage of money for anything beyond the essentials of life at Harvard. On this occasion some complimentary tickets had been provided and the pair of young undergraduates met up with some friends to attend the concert. Bernstein described the experience, "... on my right sat this unknown person, with buck teeth and a giggle and a big nose, of a charm not to be described, and when I was introduced to him and found that it was Aaron Copland ... I was blown away."

The date was November 14 – it happened to be Copland's birthday. Always quick to make friends, Bernstein was then invited to a party at the composer's apartment after the performance. There he entertained the other guests by playing Copland's Piano Variations.

Career development

Throughout his career Bernstein championed the music of Aaron Copland – especially his ballet score, *Appalachian Spring*. He described the older man as the nearest thing he ever had to a composition teacher.

Bernstein graduated from Harvard University in June 1939, aged twenty. He had earned himself a good degree, but had no real idea of where to go next. His heart was clearly set on a career in music, but he was still unsure about which of his many emerging talents he should pursue.

New York

Aware of the social and career opportunities New York had to offer, Bernstein began by sharing an apartment in New York with his lyric writer friend, Adolph Green. He also saw New York as something of a "sin city." It is likely that he felt more able to pursue his bisexuality in the liberal, artistic community. He earned what money he could by playing the piano in musical revues and cabaret engagements. When this failed to satisfy his ambitions he decided to contact Dimitri Mitropoulos

New York was always Leonard's spiritual home. It is the largest city in the United States, with a population of around seven and a half million people and, especially since the immigration of the early years of this century, has been an extraordinary melting pot of different cultures and races. Often called the Big Apple or The City That Never Sleeps, its sense of excitement and danger was well reflected in Bernstein's vibrant music.

The art of conducting

"People are constantly asking me why is a conductor necessary?" Bernstein revealed. "What does he do and why does he carry on so? Isn't the orchestra a group of highly-trained professional musicians? Don't they know how to count? Can't they read notes? Why do they need a fellow beating time for them? And, if they do, what's so glamorous about beating time can't anybody do it?"

The answer is that, while anybody might be able to do it badly, only a rare musician can do it well. Truly great conductors are few and far between – perhaps only four or five in any generation – and the special ingredient which raises a good conductor into that select few remains, for the most part, a mystery.

Some elements of conducting are clearly a matter of technique and can be taught. A modern symphony orchestra may number about one hundred players and chaos would result if each of them played a piece just as they felt. Someone must decide the speeds, the volume of each instrument so that the balance between different sections of the orchestra is correct, the way to phrase a musical line or melody and, on the most basic level, give some indication of the beat so that the orchestra can stay together and

and call on the Greek conductor's promise to help advance his prospects.

Mitropoulos and Copland agreed that Bernstein should try to develop his career as a conductor. They both helped to find him a place on the best course available at the Curtis Institute of Music in Philadelphia. The Curtis Institute failed to satisfy Bernstein for reasons that were exactly the opposite of those that limited his satisfaction with Harvard. Where Harvard had been devoted to theory, the Curtis Institute was devoted to performance. To Bernstein, it seemed intent on training its students to be excellent players without much consideration for a deep and thoughtful response to music. He remembered his time there, "As you can imagine, they regarded me as a Harvard 'smart aleck,' an intellectual bigshot, a snob and a show-off.... The school seemed to me like a virtuoso factory, turning out identical virtuosi like sausages."

Despite the isolation that he felt at the time and his later criticisms, the Curtis Institute taught him a tremendous amount about conducting. He learned that the man he had seen years before bringing Ravel's *Bolero* into existence by waving his arms around needed a technique and a degree of knowledge that it might take a lifetime to perfect.

Previous page: To the end of his life, Bernstein retained an extraordinary "presence" on the concert platform. As well as being a tremendous aural experience, his concerts had a great visual impact – both qualities guaranteeing that tickets for his performances became like gold dust for music lovers.

nobody loses their place. A conductor, therefore, must know all the instruments of the orchestra – what notes they can play and the different sounds they can make.

Love

Styles of conducting can vary dramatically. Some conductors communicate their wishes to an orchestra with the smallest of movements; some use their eyes a great deal while others prefer to keep their eyes permanently closed. Bernstein always used his entire body – sometimes leaping from the podium and, once, falling off it completely. On more than one occasion he managed to stab himself with his own baton. There can be no doubt that his style was theatrical, almost balletic, but he felt that it was always in the service of the music.

Conductors must be more than musicians, they must also be what Bernstein called "a kind of artistic historian." This means that they must know about the background to each of the composers whose music

they play – what was the atmosphere of their life and times, which other composers influenced them and what particular styles of playing are appropriate to their period?

Beyond these things, which can be gradually learned, lies the "magic" element which makes a few conductors so special. This is something that is often called "inspiration," but which Bernstein preferred to call "love." This is a mystery that can never be fully explained, but Bernstein put it like this, "The conductor must make the orchestra love the music as he loves it. It is the closest thing I know to love itself. On this current of love the conductor can communicate on the deepest level with his players and ultimately with his audience."

Curtis

Bernstein kept Helen Coates informed of his progress through the Curtis Institute – notably about his response to his new piano teacher, a formidable Russian named Isabelle Vengerova. She was very

Since the time of Mozart the orchestra has grown from some thirty players to around one hundred. The string instruments – violins, violas, cellos, and basses – form the basis of the orchestra. Behind these are the woodwind and the brass – flutes, clarinets, oboes, and bassoons add distinctive sounds, while horns, trumpets, trombones, and tubas – add bright, military tone. Finally the percussion section of drums, cymbals, and bells, produce a glorious diversity of sounds and excitement. And they are all playing at the direction of a single man – the conductor. The sense of power can be exhilarating!

29

strict on discipline and would not allow her students to question her methods. Bernstein wrote, "She scared the living daylights out of me so I left the lesson absolutely trembling!" The scare tactics obviously worked as he was soon reporting on his "astonishing progress." He worked hard, playing the piano for between three and five hours every day.

The Curtis Institute also provided Bernstein with some opportunity to study composition. One of the pieces that he wrote as an orchestration exercise was broadcast on the radio in a concert from the Institute in February 1940. This was something of a landmark in Bernstein's early career and he was especially pleased when he received a letter of congratulations from Aaron Copland.

Copland was to be the catalyst for the next important stage in Bernstein's development. He introduced Bernstein to a new mentor and "father figure," the Russian conductor of the Boston Symphony Orchestra, Serge Koussevitzky.

Tanglewood

Koussevitzky had a profound commitment to the musical education of young people and the best possible preparation of the performers of the future. The Boston Symphony Orchestra owned a country estate in New Hampshire called Tanglewood. He wanted to turn Tanglewood into the perfect environment for advanced studies and a summer home for the orchestra. Copland was to be in charge of the composition classes and Koussevitzky would be responsible for the students of conducting.

The young Bernstein was delighted when Copland offered to recommend him for the conducting class. Mitropoulos also gave his support.

That summer of 1940 was the happiest that the twenty-two year old Bernstein had ever experienced. Recalling it thirty years later he said, "I don't think we ever slept. It was so exciting! We were working all the time or playing all the time – it became the same thing." His relationship with Koussevitzky was deeply and mutually affectionate from the very start (the Russian was soon calling him "Lenushka" and

"There are many conductors in the world; many fine conductors, even some great conductors. But Koussevitzky was more: he was a great spirit."

Leonard Bernstein.

he came to call him "Koussy.") Bernstein relished the chance to learn so much about the craft of conducting at the feet of a master teacher, and he was thrilled to have so much time to gain experience conducting the resident student orchestra.

For Bernstein's first concert he conducted the Second Symphony written by his composition teacher, Randall Thompson. The response was ecstatic and Koussevitzky was the first to acknowledge that Bernstein had the makings of a great conductor.

World War II

There does not seem to have been a lot of talk of Bernstein the composer during that first exciting summer at Tanglewood. Much of the conversation, when it turned from the subject of music, was about the situation in Europe.

The war to halt the advance of Adolf Hitler's German army had begun in September 1939. By the following summer, France was under Nazi occupation, the majority of Europe was subject to German control, and Britain was threatened. The United States was not involved in the conflict, but

Between 1933 and 1945 the Hitler regime in Germany was responsible for the annihilation of more than sixteen million people in numerous concentration camps. This senseless and unforgivable murder was called the "Final Solution" by the Nazis, but it is better known by the Greek word "Holocaust," meaning the destruction of a whole people.

31

Hitler's ambitions and the threat of Japan joining the war on the side of Germany loomed. The involvement of the United States was, many thought, only a matter of time.

The sense of frustration and an eagerness to do something was greater for people like Bernstein because of the difficulties faced by Jewish people in Europe. Even before the war had begun, Hitler had selected Jewish people for especially severe treatment. By 1940 stories were reaching the United States of concentration camps where many thousands of Jewish people and others were kept under terrible conditions and then murdered.

Bernstein responded to these events with horror and quickly registered to be available to join the army should the United States enter the war.

Proud to be a Bernstein

One effect of the atmosphere of anti-Semitism at the time was that a number of Jews thought that they should change their names in order to sound more American. Koussevitzky, who saw himself as very much in the role of an alternative father to Bernstein, told him that he should change his name. "You will never see the name 'Leonard Bernstein' on a poster outside Carnegie Hall," he said.

The suggested new name was Leonard S. Burns. Bernstein, out of respect for his teacher, thought about it overnight and then announced that he was not ashamed of his name, his family, or his Jewishness and he would make it in the musical world as Leonard Bernstein or not at all.

A medical examination in 1941 established that Bernstein's lingering asthma problems from his childhood disqualified him from military service whatever happened. He responded to this news with mixed feelings. On the one hand he was relieved to discover that he would not be called upon to put his life at risk but, on the other, he felt frustrated at the prospect of not being able to fight in what he saw as such an important cause.

Inspired by his own frustrations and a desire to prove himself in other ways, rather than joining the

This famous photograph, taken in 1943, of a young Jewish boy surrendering to the Nazis in the Warsaw Ghetto shows that children were not exempt from the horror of the Holocaust. In all, 67% of the Jews in Europe were killed.

military service, Bernstein turned his attentions to composition more seriously. He had already written a certain amount of juvenilia – a young man's exploration of music. Now he began to search for a voice of his own.

True potential

Leonard Bernstein returned to the Curtis Institute for his final year, but again left without any definite idea of what he should do next. He spent some time based in Boston giving piano lessons, performing with student orchestras, and using both his network of contacts and his "chutzpah," as Jewish people describe a certain boastful cheekiness, to advance his musical career.

Although Bernstein had some limited success in conducting and playing the solo part in piano concerto performances, he also began to feel the frustration of not really fulfilling his true potential or his ambition.

On December 7, 1941, the Japanese air force bombed the United States fleet in Pearl Harbor, Hawaii, and the United States joined World War II. Most young men of Bernstein's age were soon in

The attack on the U.S. Pacific Fleet in Pearl Harbor on December 7, 1941 took place while Japanese and American officials were discussing peace in Washington. More than two thousand American servicemen were killed and a large part of the fleet was either destroyed or severely damaged.

uniform fighting for their country and he felt very self-conscious about remaining a civilian. Despite the support he received from his family and friends like Koussevitzky and Aaron Copland, Bernstein felt unsure of himself. He was dissatisfied and restless.

It was under the pressure of such circumstances that he made the decision to move back to New York. On this occasion he was able to renew his friendship with his friend from summer camp days and soon found himself sharing an apartment with Adolph Green once again.

Making a living

Money was in very short supply and Bernstein spent a lot of time earning what income he could by playing the piano in jazz clubs and for his friends' cabaret performances. Copland organized for him to earn the equivalent of a month's rent by arranging one of his own orchestral pieces, *El Salon Mexico*, on the piano. This was Bernstein's first publication. He also managed to pick up work arranging popular songs for dance bands under the name of Amber, which is the English translation of Bernstein.

All this time Bernstein was composing. First came a Sonata for Clarinet and Piano, which showed the personal and very distinctive Bernstein voice; a combination of the most important influences – jazz, Stravinsky, and Copland among them – and with something extra of his own. Bernstein also discovered that a competition was being mounted by the New England Conservatory for the composition of a piece for symphony orchestra. He saw this as an opportunity to demonstrate his practical knowledge of how the orchestra worked, as well as to write something to reflect his concern for the Jewish people in their time of danger.

Bernstein decided that his first symphony would not be entirely orchestral, but would also contain a part for a female singer – this would be the biblical words from a text about the destruction of Jerusalem, the *Lamentations of Jeremiah*. For Leonard Bernstein this text was relevant to Hitler's determination to exterminate all members of the

The hands, the eyes, and all bodily gestures of a conductor must communicate his or her feelings about the music to the musicians. Bernstein's concentration and commitment were always total.

Jewish faith. The *Jeremiah Symphony*, as it became known, is still played to this day as Leonard Bernstein's first masterpiece.

"God said, 'Take Bernstein'"

The *Jeremiah Symphony* did not win the competition, but the piece that did is lost to history. Bernstein was disappointed and felt the failure bitterly for a short time, but he was soon distracted by other considerations. The division between his attraction to composition and to conducting was about to take its most momentous turn.

Serge Koussevitzky knew that the New York Philharmonic Orchestra was looking for someone to act as assistant conductor to its musical director, Artur Rodzinski, and suggested Bernstein as a candidate. The position was in no way as glamorous as it sounded. The job of an assistant conductor often involves nothing more exciting than sitting in the hall and advising the conductor on matters of acoustics or making sure that all of the players have the correctly marked parts for a rehearsal. It does, however, provide a wonderful opportunity to learn many of the practicalities of conducting. It is also a position that involves always being available to substitute for a conductor who is not able to direct a concert for reasons of ill health.

While Bernstein waited for news from the New York Philharmonic, he was invited to Pittsburgh to conduct the first performance of the *Jeremiah Symphony*. The première was a tremendous success, not least because the message of the piece was so appropriate to the times. Bernstein dedicated the work to his father, and other orchestras soon hurried to include it in their performances.

Meanwhile, coinciding with Bernstein's twenty-fifth birthday in August 1943, Rodzinski reached a decision about who should be appointed as his assistant. He did so with a quotation to the press that has become part of musical mythology, "I have gone through all the conductors I know of in my mind and I finally asked God whom I should take and God said, 'Take Bernstein.'"

"I am a public person when I conduct, and a private person when I compose. I take on a whole new personality."
Leonard Bernstein.

The idea of the family is central to the Jewish faith and perhaps no more so than in the relationship between father and son. Leonard's father did not at first support his son's ambitions, but, when success began to come, he was pleased to describe Leonard as "my gift to Uncle Sam!"

35

Even with this rather unlikely backing, Leonard Bernstein could only guess at the triumph which was just around the corner. It would herald the beginning of his world famous conducting career.

Total immersion

His appointment as assistant conductor of one of the United States' top orchestras gave Bernstein the opportunity to attend rehearsals and witness how a variety of conductors achieved their success. It was an enviable chance to learn the orchestral repertoire at the closest possible quarters.

Since a small apartment above Carnegie Hall came with the position, Bernstein found himself literally living on the job and he relished every moment of it. He was able to retire from assisting rehearsals to dream about the possibility of actually standing on the podium and conducting the orchestra in a concert himself.

However busy he was attending to the needs of the New York Philharmonic, Bernstein did not neglect his composing. He had written a witty series of songs called *I Hate Music* and had arranged a performance to be given by the famous French singer, Jennie Tourell, in the New York Town Hall one Saturday in November 1943. This was such an important achievement that the Bernstein family was invited down from Boston to attend the concert.

The songs were a great success and even Bernstein's father, Sam, who had been somewhat reluctant to make the trip was pleased to see that his son's name was beginning to be well known in New York musical circles. There was a party after the concert and Bernstein was so delighted by his triumph that he had rather a lot to drink. Early on Sunday morning, Bernstein was woken from his sleep to be told through his hangover that the conductor of that afternoon's Philharmonic concert was unwell and therefore unlikely to be able to make the performance.

Debut

This was the opportunity that any young conductor in Bernstein's position both wanted and feared. If such a thing happens at all in the career of a musician, it happens only once. Bernstein's first thought was how he could clear his head. His second thought was panic!

He managed to do a number of essential things – he contacted his family and told them not to return to Boston, he visited the conductor to discuss the pieces to be played in the concert, and he went to a pharmacist to get some medication to help him through such an unexpected and traumatic afternoon.

In the middle of the afternoon of November 14, 1943, twenty-five year old Leonard Bernstein stood in the wings of the great concert hall and surveyed his position. He had never faced a professional orchestra in concert like this before and he would become the youngest person to conduct the

Opposite: Carnegie Hall opened in 1891 as New York's most important concert hall. It was named after the Scottish-born industrialist who had made himself a millionaire by developing the American iron and steel industry. It was the place where all musicians most wanted to perform.

Below: Leonard Bernstein's energetic personality and theatrical style of conducting attracted much attention. This sketch tries to capture the excitement of his performances that ensured that he always had a full audience.

Throughout his life, Bernstein wallowed in the admiration of his public and came to expect "red carpet" treatment wherever he went. Some critics saw this as a sign of his arrogance, but the more perceptive, and those closer to him, recognized it as compensation for a deeper sense of insecurity.

Philharmonic. He decided, at that moment, that he had earned the opportunity that lay ahead of him by virtue of his talent and he was not, therefore, going to rely on medication. He threw away his pills and walked proudly out onto the conductor's podium.

The concert was broadcast across the United States on live radio and, when he walked off in a daze at the end, Bernstein was met with a telegram from Koussevitzky saying, "I'm listening now and it's wonderful." Leonard Bernstein was famous!

Only the beginning

The day after the unexpected debut performance with the New York Philharmonic, the newspapers proclaimed Bernstein as a new American hero. The *New York Times* had the news of his performance on the front page. The *New York Daily News* chose an image from baseball to describe Bernstein's opportunity and his success, "A shoe-string catch in center field. Make it and you're a hero. Muff-it and you're a dope. He made it!"

Of course, it was only the beginning. Now Bernstein had to prove that he was more than just an overnight sensation. It was exactly the break he needed and he was eager to meet the expectations as

"Lenny had a natural inclination for the spotlight; he never hid his light under a bushel. . . . He was magnetic, outgoing, fun-loving, surrounded himself with many friends and had an abundance of acquaintances from all walks of life."

*Mildred Spiegel,
a friend from Harvard.*

the United States' first conductor of great potential that landed on his shoulders that Monday morning.

Bernstein was never short of energy throughout his life, but this early success gave him a tremendous boost. He was conscious of his musical skills as a whole and worked incredibly long hours to make sure that his life as a composer was not neglected by the demands of his new conducting career.

"On the Town"

In 1944, Bernstein met the dancer and choreographer, Jerome Robbins. Together they worked on producing Bernstein's first ballet, *Fancy Free*. This tells the story of three sailors who have a short time ashore before they have to return to their ship. It was a particularly appropriate storyline for a nation at war.

Bernstein was persuaded by his friend Adolph Green that there was a good chance of writing a Broadway musical based on the same subject. Working with Green's partner, Betty Comden, they produced the first of Bernstein's great musicals, *On the Town*. The

Gene Kelly, Frank Sinatra, and Jules Munshin star as the three sailors with only twenty-four hours to enjoy New York to the utmost, in the famous movie of On the Town. *Described by one critic as "a peach of a show," it cemented Bernstein's love affair with his adopted city.*

result proved to be the start of Bernstein's three tributes to the city he loved, New York.

The sailors in the musical have only twenty-four hours to experience the Big Apple to the full. They fall in and out of love and get involved in confusing situations. Bernstein's music is full of lively jazz songs and dances as well as some touching slow ballads. It was a fantastic success – Leonard Bernstein could do no wrong. When the show was made into a movie five years later, Frank Sinatra turned one of its best songs, "New York, New York" into a popular hit in its own right.

Wasting his time?

After the triumph of *On the Town*, Bernstein was quickly returned to earth by the conflicting demands of composition and conducting that would plague him throughout his life.

One of the first to claim that he was wasting his time by writing "tunes for the masses" was Koussevitzky. Various factors played their part in Bernstein's response. Among them was the fact that money was to be made in the sphere of musicals. He was also eager not to be limited by the arguments between popular and serious music.

"It is impossible for me to make an exclusive choice among the various activities of conducting, symphonic composition, writing for the theater and playing the piano. What seems right for me at any given moment is what I must do...," Bernstein explained. The important thing was that, whatever area of music he concentrated on, he demonstrated a genius that nobody dared to question.

Everybody wanted a bit of his dynamism and he found himself in demand not only throughout the United States, but also in Europe. In 1946 Bernstein conducted concerts of American music, including Gershwin's *Rhapsody in Blue* in Prague to celebrate the newly-liberated Czechoslovakia and then moved on to further triumphs with the London Philharmonic Orchestra in Britain.

Back home in New York, Bernstein worked again with the choreographer Jerome Robbins on a new ballet, *Facsimile,* which dealt with the individual's isolation in a modern world of increasing technology. As it happened, isolation was soon pushed to the back of Bernstein's mind when he met a beautiful young actress from Chile.

The many languages of love

As an attractive and successful young man, Bernstein had many admirers, men as well as women. After a concert in February 1946, Leonard Bernstein met a woman with whom he hoped he would spend the rest of his life.

Felicia Montealegre Cohn was on the eve of her twenty-fourth birthday when she met Leonard Bernstein and the two were immediately attracted to each other. She had youthful South American beauty, an infectious charm that endeared her to everybody, and quite importantly she was half-Jewish.

Despite having a small part in a Broadway play, Felicia's English was far from perfect and Leonard took special delight in giving her lessons in English grammar. His conducting career took him away from New York for a large part of the summer of 1946 but,

Opposite: New York – famous mostly for its energy and raucous fun. Bernstein's musical On the Town *also acknowledges that pleasure can pass all too quickly and that places like the Big Apple can easily become, a "Lonely Town."*

Bernstein and his wife, who was born Felicia Montealegre Cohn in Costa Rica in 1922. The two were deeply in love, but Felicia, like the partners of so many international superstars, had to accept long periods of her husband's absence. Her own career as an actress never really achieved its early promise, but she had a great success taking the speaking role in the American première of Bernstein's Kaddish Symphony *in Boston in 1964. Despite his affairs, Leonard knew that Felicia was the one great love of his life. Her death in June 1978, due to cancer, was a blow from which he never really recovered.*

late in the year, he was writing to Helen Coates about the prospect of marriage, "She's an angel and a beautiful companion. I shouldn't be surprised if it worked out beautifully in the end."

Israel

Nineteen forty-seven was a busy year of touring for Bernstein and the composing side of his career was, again, rather neglected. The most important event of the year was an invitation to conduct in Palestine – the biblical homeland of the Jewish race. Palestine had taken on even greater significance after the extermination of some six million Jewish people by the Nazis during World War II.

At this time the area was still under the "protection" of the British government, but was soon to become the independent state of Israel. There was a lot of resistance against Britain from the Arab population in the region and it was far from being a safe place to travel. Bernstein was determined that fears for his personal safety would not interfere with his wish to show support for his religion. His father, Sam Bernstein, went with him and was overjoyed

Bernstein playing with the Israel Philharmonic Orchestra in the biblical town of Beersheba. Like many Jewish people, Leonard was committed to the idea of a national homeland for the members of his faith. This, historically, had to be in Palestine, which was also called the Holy Land because of its links with Judaism, Christianity, and Islam.

to see his son succeed in such a holy place.

The Palestine Symphony Orchestra was made up of some of the world's finest musicians who had escaped or survived World War II. At the first rehearsal, Bernstein was furious to find members of the orchestra talking among themselves whenever he gave an instruction. But he was profoundly moved when he discovered that, because the players had no common language, they were translating his wishes from one to another – through Hebrew, German, Russian, and Polish. The concerts, which included Bernstein's own *Jeremiah Symphony,* were an overwhelming triumph with over four thousand people at one performance.

Anxiety

The authorities in Israel were so impressed by Bernstein's easy rapport with the orchestra that they wanted him to become its first music director. Bernstein was greatly flattered, but refused. He was convinced that his future lay in the United States and in following his mentor, Koussevitzky, who was due to retire from the Boston Symphony Orchestra.

Bernstein always said that he felt most relaxed when he was in the Boston area of his youth and nothing would have been more satisfying than to become the first American-born director of the Boston orchestra. Despite having the full support of Koussevitzky, the political considerations can outweigh the artistic and the job finally went to a Frenchman, Charles Munch.

Meanwhile Leonard's relationship with Felicia deteriorated – partly because of the amount of time he spent going across the United States as a guest-conductor and also because the admiration Leonard received from fans wherever he went made them both wonder if he could ever be content with her alone. They decided to call off their engagement.

Against this background, Bernstein began to work on a new symphony. He had been much impressed by his reading of the English poet W. H. Auden and decided to name his new piece after one of Auden's collections, *The Age of Anxiety.*

Top: The Jewish state of Israel was proclaimed on May 14, 1948 by a decree of the United Nations. A massive immigration into the area of holocaust survivors and their families from Europe began (above). A series of Arab-Israeli wars followed and the entire region has remained one of the most volatile in the world.

43

The symphony does not follow the poem in detail but shares its theme of people facing loneliness and trying to find their idea of happiness and their search for God. Bernstein described its opening, for two solo clarinets, as "the loneliest music I know." Other sections are very close to jazz themes and the influence of composers including Gustav Mahler, can be heard throughout.

The piano plays an important part all through the piece and some people thought that it was more like a piano concerto than a symphony, but Bernstein was happy with his choice of title. The work is dedicated to "Koussy" who conducted the first performance with Bernstein playing the piano part.

A death and a marriage

In 1951, the Israel Philharmonic made its first visit to the United States with Leonard Bernstein and Serge Koussevitzky sharing the conducting. Bernstein decided that, after the tour, he would take a sabbatical – a year away from his heavy conducting commitments – to concentrate on composition.

He resumed his relationship with Felicia and their engagement was back on. They rented a house together in Mexico and Leonard was working on new projects in idyllic surroundings when the shattering news arrived from Boston that his friend and mentor Koussevitzky was on his deathbed.

Serge Koussevitzky was not only a musical mentor for Leonard, but also something of a father figure. At a speech in "Koussy's" memory, Bernstein said, "It was at his feet that we learned contemporary music and its indispensable part in musical life. He was the great educator . . . through it all, he taught us one elemental and indestructible lesson: the composer comes first!" This was true of Leonard himself who so clearly set out to shadow and develop his mentor's ideals.

Leonard dashed back to spend some hours with Koussy before he died. It was a shattering blow.

Bernstein gave a tearful speech at the funeral. He had inherited a great tradition of music from "Koussy," as he fondly called Koussevitzky, which he was proud to be able to continue. He also inherited a pair of "Koussy's" cufflinks, which from that time on Bernstein always wore for conducting. He would kiss them superstitiously before each concert.

As a further act of respect, Leonard wore one of Koussevitzky's white suits when he and Felicia were married with full Jewish ritual on September 9, 1951.

Working and family

The half dozen years that followed the Bernsteins' marriage were the most musically productive and commercially successful of Leonard's composing life. He continued to tour the United States, Europe, and Israel as a conductor. He began to make television documentaries and he still found time to write three more Broadway musicals. In addition he and Felicia had their first two children. His first daughter, Jamie, was born in 1952 and the son he longed for, Alexander, in 1955. At the time he was

Leonard at home in New York, 1961, with Felicia and his first two children, Jamie and Alexander. His third child, Nina, was born the following year. Leonard doted on his children and especially loved to teach them singing and musical games while they were still very young. Of course, they missed him greatly when he was away on tour, particularly at "booze times" – that hour in the evening when Leonard would reach for his first drink and really begin to relax!

The glorious team of true collaborators who came together so successfully to produce the great American musical. Leonard with the inevitable cigarette, Jerome Robbins who choreographed the wonderful dances of West Side Story, *and the lyric writing partnership of Betty Comden and Adolph Green. It was their ability to work so well together – without any jealousies and with so much exuberant fun – that guaranteed their success.*

trying very hard to make the most of his new role as a loving, devoted father.

The first of the three musicals, *Wonderful Town*, was written in less than five weeks under rather peculiar circumstances. A producer had already commissioned a musical based on a play and successful movie, *My Sister Eileen*. About five weeks before rehearsals were due to begin, everyone involved in the production of the show decided that the music was not as good as they expected. Bernstein was asked to help improve some of the show's songs.

Bernstein refused this offer, but said that he would be happy to write the entire musical as long as he could work with his friends Betty Comden and Adolph Green, who wrote the lyrics for *On the Town*. They were soon joined by the choreographer, Jerome Robbins, in the second of their musical "love letters" to New York City.

The story concerns two sisters, Ruth and Eileen, who come to New York to achieve their ambitions to become a writer and an actress. Things do not go to plan and they find themselves leading a poor life in New York's artistic quarter, Greenwich Village. Happily, love and chance intervene to provide a suitably upbeat ending. The musical score is full of fun and includes a Brazilian conga and the sweetly sentimental ballad, "A Little Bit in Love."

Wonderful Town won a number of awards as the Best Musical of the Season and ran for 559 performances on Broadway.

"Candide"

Before his next musical, which had a more difficult "birth," Bernstein composed the music for the movie, *On the Waterfront* starring Marlon Brando. Bernstein had previously resisted offers to write for Hollywood because he saw the music as being too secondary to the action on the screen. On this occasion, however, he agreed to look at the movie and was so impressed that he said, "I heard music as I watched. That was enough." The movie won eight Oscars.

Candide was a project on a much grander scale and one much closer to Bernstein's heart. Bernstein had been captivated by Voltaire's short novel, *Candide,* when he was still a student at Harvard. He liked the way it made fun of serious ideas about religion and was thrilled at the prospect of turning it into a musical.

Bernstein's chief colleague on *Candide* was a playwright named Lillian Hellman and history has put much of the blame for the show's initial lack of success on her shoulders. It was said that she failed to realize that the story was a comedy. By the 1989 performance in London, the problems had been solved by the input of many other writers and it had become a generally acknowledged masterpiece.

Marlon Brando starred in the movie On the Waterfront – *Bernstein's only music score written especially for a movie. The story concerns an ex-boxer (Brando) who first works for a corrupt union boss but, after the murder of his brother and with the encouragement of his priest and girlfriend, he changes sides and joins the other dock workers to fight for a fairer system. Bernstein's music was nominated for an Oscar and he later arranged some of the themes into a successful Symphonic Suite.*

Long and lasting

The story is a seemingly foolish one. The young man, Candide, is persuaded by his teacher Dr. Pangloss, that the world we have is the best of all possible worlds. After a series of adventures, which

Above and opposite: West Side Story *is a show absolutely bursting with tension and nowhere more so than in its brilliant dance sequences. The "chemistry" that existed between Bernstein and his choreographer, Jerome Robbins, was the single most important element in the musical's success and subsequent popularity. The wordless, opening section consists solely of Leonard's music and the frenzied dancing of the two gangs – to establish the tragic conflict at the heart of the story.*

include an earthquake in Lisbon, an execution by the forces of the Spanish Inquisition, and a disastrous visit to Latin America in search of the legendary gold of El Dorado, he comes to realize that life is much more limited and the best thing is to accept the rough with the smooth and make the best of the reality of life in simple ways.

The music is full of references to Viennese waltzes, Spanish rhythms, and Gilbert and Sullivan operetta. A number of the individual songs became popular very quickly especially "Glitter and be Gay," which is sung by Candide's girlfriend, Cunegonde.

The final form of *Candide* only became public near the end of Bernstein's life, but history may find that this was the work where he was at the height of his powers as a composer combining classical and popular styles into a lasting theatrical masterwork.

"West Side Story"

The third Bernstein musical of the 1950s was one that guaranteed Bernstein a permanent place in the world of popular musicals.

> *"In 1957, <u>West Side Story</u> set a new standard for Broadway musicals. Leonard Bernstein, at the pinnacle of his career, produced a fast-moving, muscular masterpiece."*
>
> Humphrey Burton, from the Sunday Times, *1994.*

He once admitted that he was very sensitive to the accusation of never having written a true hit song. "It would be nice to hear someone accidentally whistle something of mine, somewhere, just once," he said. After he had written *West Side Story* that was something he would never have to worry about ever again, wherever he went in the world.

The original idea came from the choreographer Jerome Robbins who suggested a musical based on Shakespeare's *Romeo and Juliet* set in contemporary New York and involving a conflict between Jewish people and Catholics back in 1949. Bernstein was enthusiastic, but had no time to pursue the project.

By the time the idea came around again in the 1950s, the Shakespeare connection remained, but the conflict was to be between a gang of self-styled "Americans" and a group of immigrant Hispanic Puerto Ricans. There was to be a girl from one side of the dispute and a boy from the other. As in *Romeo and Juliet*, their love was to be frustrated and eventually destroyed by the war between their two "families." Despite the tragedy of death, this brings about a final reconciliation between the two gangs.

Following page: The Sharks meet the Jets in West Side Story. *Set against the tension of gang warfare, a love affair develops. Natalie Wood (inset) plays the part of Maria, whose role is based on Shakespeare's Juliet. In the famous "balcony scene" she meets her Romeo – in this case Tony – and at the height of their love, and full of optimism about their relationship, they sing a great love duet, "Tonight."*

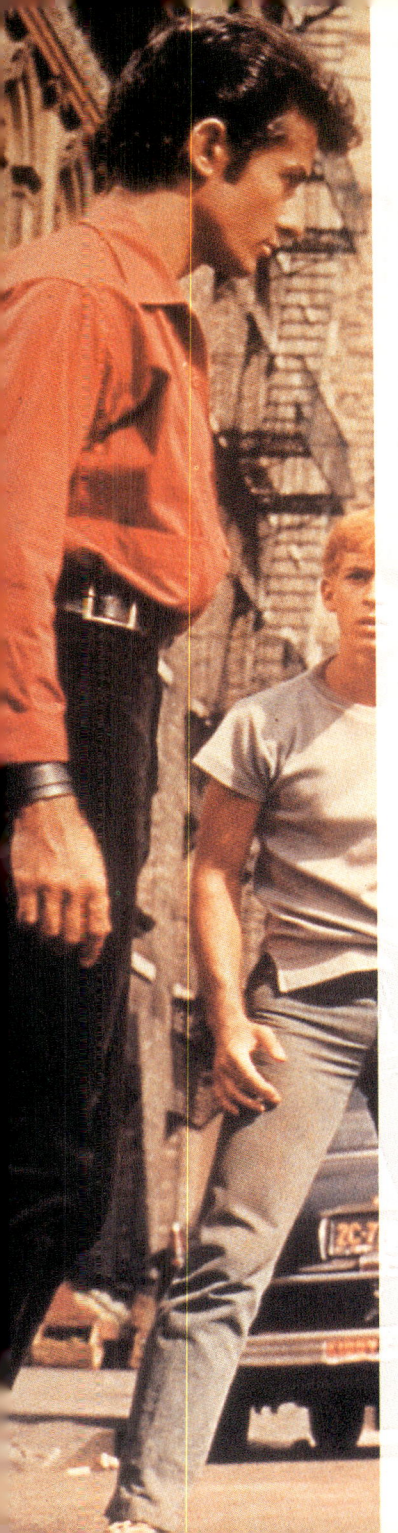

Bernstein kept a diary of the development of the musical. In August 1955 he wrote, "Suddenly it all springs to life. I hear rhythms and pulses and – most of all – I can sort of feel the form." What was needed was a writer who could work with Bernstein on the lyrics for his songs and who would share his enthusiasm for the project.

Making a legend

The final and essential member of the *West Side Story* team was the lyricist Stephen Sondheim. Bernstein was delighted to be working with someone who was not only a writer of lyrics, but also enough of a musician to understand the composer's considerations. In the end, the tremendous and lasting success of *West Side Story* can only be explained by the brilliance of the combination of music, words, and dance.

West Side Story was always going to be based on the energy of its youthful characters, so when it came to casting the parts for its first performance there was no point in looking for famous actors or singers. The show had to be the star, not its performers. It is for this reason that so many school and youth groups throughout the world continue to mount productions using actors even younger than those intended by the show's creators. It seems that there are always plenty of conflicts and problems in adolescent relationships to keep the story relevant and fresh.

Doubts?

At the time of its writing, however, there were many people who had doubts about its success. Bernstein was later able to write with a smile, "Everybody told us to stop. They all said it was suicidal... how could we do a musical... that's so filled with hatefulness and ugliness?" In the story the two main characters are Tony and Maria. Tony was one of the founders of the American gang, the Jets, and Maria is the sister of the leader of the Puerto Rican gang, the Sharks.

Tony and Maria meet and fall in love against the background of the violent hatred between the two

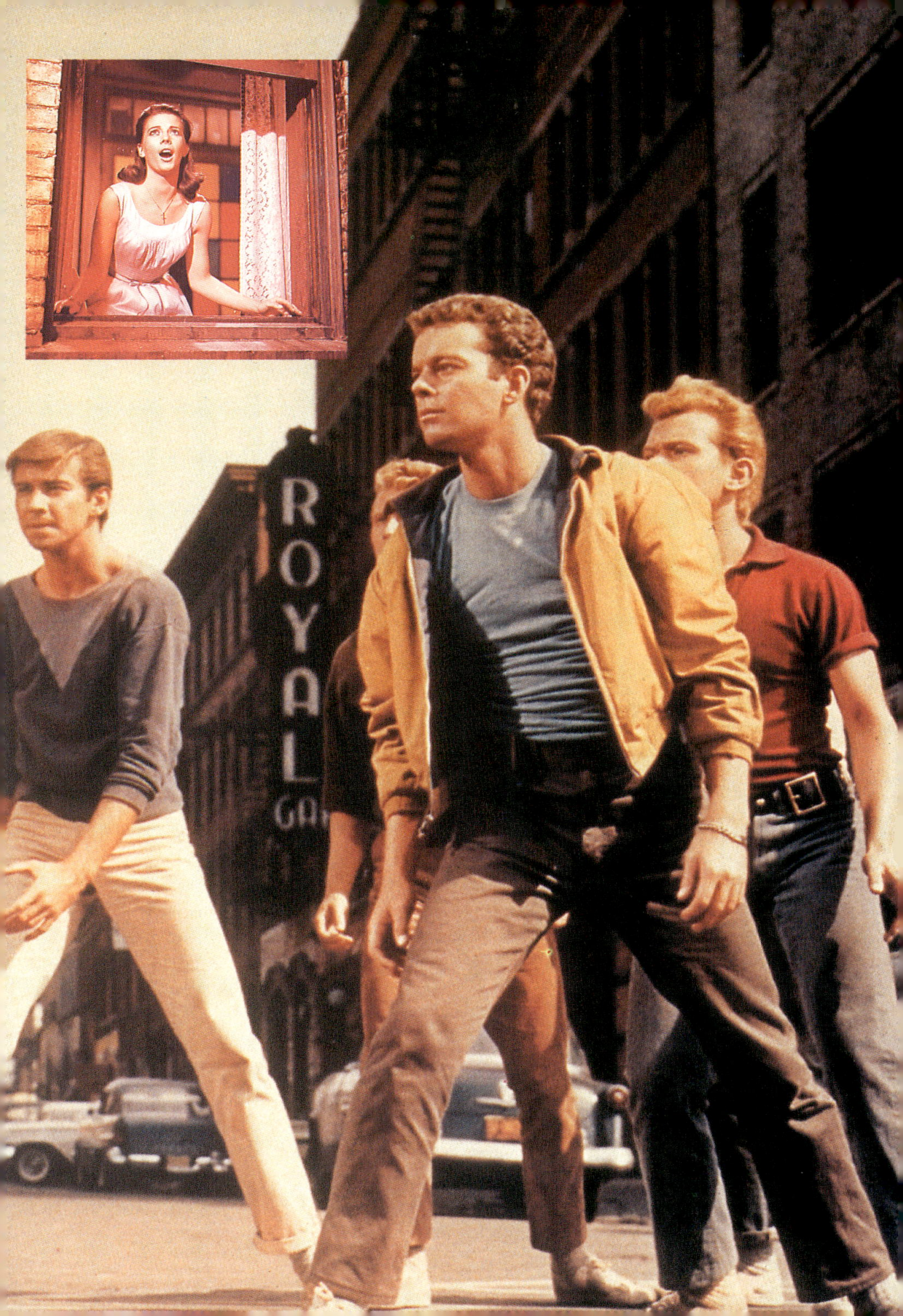
ROYAL

Natalie Wood and Richard Beymer (Tony) act out a touching mock wedding ceremony in the central section of West Side Story. *The two lovers promise eternal devotion to each other in the song "One Hand, One Heart," and Tony agrees to do all he can to put an end to the gang warfare that stands between them and complete happiness. It is while he is trying to do so that Maria's brother is accidentally killed, and all hopes for the teenage romance darken as the show comes to its tragic conclusion.*

opposing gangs. Tony, who wants to put the gang warfare behind him, accidentally kills Maria's brother and is then hunted down and killed by a member of the Sharks. Maria is left, without the love of her life, or her brother, to point to the uselessness and destruction of all such violence.

Many of the songs from the musical have become popular standards in their own right. They are often sung and recorded by a variety of performers in different arrangements. Among the most famous are "Maria," "Somewhere," "America," and "Tonight." These are melodies that are known and loved by musicians of all styles all over the world. *West Side Story* played for a year and a half on Broadway and firmly cemented Leonard Bernstein's reputation as a great and greatly-loved composer. It also made him a lot of money, especially after the movie was released in 1961.

"The Joy of Music"

By 1958, Bernstein had become something of a musical god to the American public. To add to the triumph of his popular scores and Broadway successes, he was finally awarded the position of musical director of the New York Philharmonic Orchestra and so became the first American-born conductor to lead one of his country's greatest and most famous orchestras.

He was forty and he was determined to be the most youthful of music-makers. His great project was to introduce young people to classical music and he was delighted to exploit the new medium of television to do this. He began a series of "Young People's Concerts" that were broadcast weekly on television across the United States. He explored, in a relaxed, untechnical way, the history of musical development from the time of Bach to the present day. These shows have been made available on video and, due to their popularity, are regularly repeated. They introduced a whole generation of children to classical music. Bernstein also wrote a book, *The Joy of Music*. He was at his pinnacle as composer, conductor, and educator.

The showman

Bernstein relished every opportunity to be the main focus of attention. His conducting style had always been flamboyant and he made no apologies for this. As far as he was concerned, if he felt the music so deeply that at certain moments he had to jump in the air to express his emotion, then so be it.

In 1959 he had the chance to demonstrate his showmanship to an entirely new audience when he took his orchestra, the New York Philharmonic, on a tour of the Soviet Union. This was at the height of the Cold War when relations between the United States and Russia were very tense. The audiences for Bernstein's concerts took him to their hearts.

Leonard Bernstein became a father again with the birth of his second daughter, Nina, in 1962. Despite the continued temptation of casual – especially homosexual – affairs, he wanted only to be an ideal husband and father. However, his love of flattery and his desire to "drink-deep" of life's potential experiences began to put too great a strain on his marriage. But Felicia's sense of devotion – to husband and young family – kept the couple together for the time being.

A symphony for the president

Bernstein had already begun to work on ideas for a third symphony when, in November 1963, not only the United States, but the entire world was thrown

In his book, Conductor's World, *David Wooldridge writes, "Whatever criticisms may be levelled against Bernstein's antics on the podium and extraordinary tactics in rehearsal, he is a figure whom it is impossible to ignore. . . . It remains beyond dispute that Bernstein fulfils the prime. . . function of any conductor in bringing the music abundantly to life."*

"He was from the outset a showman, mocked by critics for clapping to cue clashing cymbals, but he was also a man inhabited by music, capable of endless hours of intense concentration, and above all, of communicating his passion and energy to other musicians."

*John Wells,
from* The Daily Telegraph, *1994.*

53

Leonard Bernstein's already established fame was confirmed once again when he appeared on the cover of the popular American magazine Time.

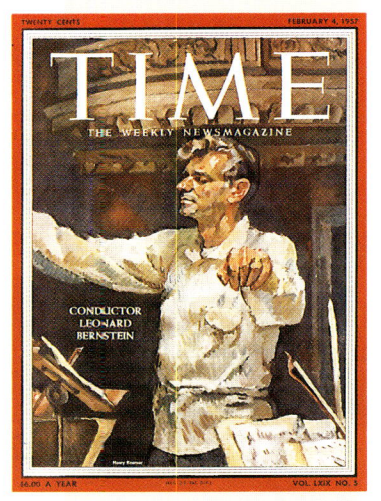

into a state of shock by news of the assassination of President John F. Kennedy.

Bernstein had been a guest at the White House in Washington and was a keen supporter of the young president's liberal policies. He felt the loss on a personal, as well as a national, level. Two days after the killing he conducted a memorial performance of Mahler's *Resurrection Symphony* in New York. It was a profoundly moving tribute and a statement of belief in the future. He said of the late president, "In mourning him, we must be worthy of him."

The third symphony was to become a further tribute. He called it *Kaddish* – the name of the Jewish prayers that commemorate the dead – and he dedicated the work to the memory of Kennedy. It has parts for adult and children's choirs and a speaker who narrates a text that Bernstein wrote himself. The speaker disputes with God asking how he could allow the miseries of the world to continue, but the work ends with a feeling of reconciliation and hope for the future. It was given a notable first performance in Israel, but has never gained the popularity of its predecessors.

Slow down

After *Kaddish,* Bernstein accepted what his friends had been telling him for some time – he was doing too much and needed to slow down and rest. Not only the pressure of work, but his general lifestyle, especially his constant cigarette smoking, was beginning to have a bad effect on his health. Everybody nagged him to quit the habit, but he couldn't – or wouldn't.

Bernstein decided to have a year away from the New York Philharmonic in order to devote his time to other projects. Among these were conducting Verdi's *Falstaff* at the Metropolitan Opera in New York and working on a new piece of religious music which had been commissioned by the Anglican cathedral at Chichester in southern England. Bernstein was intrigued by the prospect of writing for a large choir, which would consist only of men and boys – the traditional English cathedral sound.

He chose to set to music fragments of the biblical Psalms of David in Hebrew. The result was *Chichester Psalms* – a work of serene innocence that became his most popular and frequently performed non-Broadway work.

The cathedral authorities who asked him to write the piece had said they would be delighted to find a "hint of *West Side Story* about the music." Bernstein obliged by composing some of his best melodies. When the work was played in New York, a critic described it as, "extremely direct and simple and very beautiful."

A new orchestra to love

There have been many arguments about whether London or New York is the musical capital of the world. These are usually based on performance – the best orchestras and opera houses, the most concerts. There is, however, no dispute about which is the capital city of musical history. It can only be Vienna – home to the triumphs of Mozart, Schubert, Beethoven, Brahms, and Bernstein's hero, Gustav Mahler.

When Bernstein was first invited to conduct the Vienna Philharmonic Orchestra in 1966, he was dubious. He felt that many of the players may have a past tainted by association with Hitler's Nazi party. On the other hand, he knew that they had a tradition of playing the masterpieces of music which stretched back to the composers themselves. It was the

The Vienna Philharmonic Orchestra was founded by the composer and conductor, Otto Nicolai in 1842. As well as giving purely symphonic concerts, it is the orchestra of the Vienna Opera House. Famous for the luxurious, velvet-like "sheen" of its string sound and its wealth of musical tradition, it is watched by millions on television every New Year's Day when a special concert of Viennese music is broadcast live around the world. Initially, Bernstein was overawed at the prospect of conducting this world-famous orchestra, in 1966, but as with most experiences, he took it all in his stride!

world's "classiest" orchestra and he could not resist the temptation.

Bernstein would later tell a story about the Vienna Philharmonic. He was conducting some music by the Viennese composer Richard Strauss. After the rehearsal a player came to him and told him about a particular traditional way of playing a waltz in Vienna. "Ach so!" said Bernstein. A few minutes later another player came to tell him about their special tradition, but this time it was something completely different.

At the next rehearsal Bernstein addressed the orchestra, "Now everybody shut up. I have heard much too much about Viennese waltzes and nobody seems to agree with anybody. So we will do it my way and whatever I do – you follow!" Follow him they did – and continued to do so, with great mutual love and respect, in numerous concerts and recordings for the next twenty-five years.

Bereavement

In the late 1960s, Bernstein was happy to tell journalists that he was married to the New York Philharmonic and, therefore, only having something of an illicit affair with the Vienna orchestra. The truth was a little different.

Bernstein knew that his international reputation was secured. Concerns about his health were doubled when it was realized that he had problems with his heart as well as with his breathing. It was clear even to the workaholic Bernstein that he needed to offload as many responsibilities as possible. He decided to resign his position as musical director of the New York Philharmonic.

In June 1968, Senator Robert Kennedy, brother of the late president, was assassinated in Los Angeles. Bernstein was asked to be responsible for the music at the state funeral. He was proud to accept. The following year brought a much more personal bereavement. His father, Sam, had been in poor health for some time and finally lost his battle against heart disease at the end of April 1969. Leonard was devastated by the death of his father.

"Composer, conductor, pianist, teacher classicist, and popularizer, as much at home with the Broadway musical as on the operatic stage and the symphony orchestra podium, Leonard Bernstein was an innovator who risked his prodigious talents in many directions, a truly American phenomenon who appeared all over the world in the half century he spent with music."

From Bernstein Remembered.

He re-scheduled as many of his concerts as possible to include the *Jeremiah Symphony,* which had been dedicated to his father.

A piece for the Lord

Leonard Bernstein was the best musical friend of the Kennedy family. When it was decided that a new Center for the Performing Arts was to be opened in Washington, dedicated to the memory of President John F. Kennedy, it was only natural that Bernstein should be invited to write a piece for its opening.

The work that resulted was the last of Bernstein's theatrical compositions. He called it *Mass*: "A Piece for Singers, Players, and Dancers." It divided the critics at the time of its first performance and has continued to do so. Like *Kaddish,* it questions God's authority before accepting His wisdom and power. Musically, it includes folk and pop music, classical sections, jazz, and theatrical devices that would not have been out of place on Broadway. It is a total combination of all the compositional skills that Bernstein possessed. At the end, a boys' choir fills the aisles and brings the touch of peace to the audience, saying with each touch: "Pass it on." It was a statement of Leonard's religious, political, and musical philosophy.

The first performance was given on September 8, 1971. Despite the fact it was given few further performances, Bernstein regarded it as among his finest offerings and it remains the single work which still has to find its true recognition as one of his major contributions to twentieth-century music.

Leonard Bernstein with Jacqueline Onassis, former wife of the late President Kennedy, at a performance of Mass *in the recently opened John F. Kennedy Center for the Performing Arts in Washington in 1972.*

Professor Bernstein

After the first performance of *Mass*, Bernstein had many opportunities to contemplate the passage of time. Now aged fifty-three, he conducted his one thousandth performance with the New York Philharmonic. He was now its "Lifetime Laureate Conductor" without responsibilities for the administration.

Nineteen seventy-three saw Bernstein invited back to his old university, Harvard, to deliver a series of lectures that were televised across the United States,

Opposite and next page: Leonard Bernstein thought that music expressed the most profound experiences. In his later years he re-recorded the symphonies of Gustav Mahler – whose music meant so much to him. Of the concluding section of Mahler's Ninth Symphony Bernstein said, "Take the last page . . . which comes closest among anything in all arts . . . to portraying the act of dying, the actual experience of letting go, little by little." His last few months enabled him to test this belief against his own experience of "letting go."
Below: Severe fits of coughing and shortness of breath were constant interruptions to Leonard's over taxing schedule as the years went on.

Europe, and much of the rest of the world. In them, Bernstein tried to cover the whole history of music and relate its development to that of speech. Students and teachers waited anxiously for a place in the audience for his lectures that were later published as *The Unanswered Question*.

Although it felt strange to be back at his old college, Bernstein was delighted to be given such a prestigious opportunity to share his knowledge and his thoughts about the significance of music. "Everything I do is, in one way or another, teaching," he told his audience. His skill as a teacher was outstanding and those present felt privileged to learn from such a distinguished, albeit chain-smoking, professor.

A difficult time

By 1976, the Bernstein's marriage was in trouble. Leonard had never solved the problem of his own sexuality and he separated from Felicia and the three children to live with a male lover. However, when it was found that Felicia had cancer, they were reconciled.

In January 1977, Bernstein conducted his last major composition to commemorate the inauguration of President Carter. This was *Songfest* – a setting for orchestra and six singers of a series of poems that describe the identity of American history. It was to prove his final undisputed masterpiece.

After a series of breathing problems, Bernstein was diagnosed as suffering from a heart complaint. When it became obvious that Felicia's remaining time was limited, the extent of Leonard's guilt was overwhelming. After a year, Felicia died.

After Felicia's death, Leonard took to his bed for weeks on end. A few months after his bereavement he had to attend the gala concert which celebrated his sixtieth birthday. He described it as, "One of the worst nights of my life. One of the most touching too, because everybody came. . . . But it was horrible because I had to smile and be gracious when, inside, I was feeling rock bottom." He never fully recovered from the shock of Felicia's death.

From that time on Leonard Bernstein, who had seemed close to immortal, showed all the signs of his age and physical decline.

Citizen of the world

For Leonard Bernstein's many admirers, friends, and associates, it was almost impossible to imagine that such a dynamic character could ever suffer from anything so mundane as a limited life span.

Bernstein himself often refused to acknowledge that his body was protesting against the strain of the pressures that his career was putting upon it. He relied on his cigarettes, his fondness for a drink, and any pills he could persuade doctors to prescribe.

He continued to compose as much as he could, but his main work from the 1980s was a song collection. *Arias and Barcarolles* is a tender tribute to family life – the type of life that Bernstein's commitment to his career and driving ambition deprived him of.

As Bernstein entered his seventies, he was generally regarded as the world's leading conductor. When a concert was planned to celebrate the destruction of the Berlin Wall in 1989, Bernstein was the obvious choice to lead a performance of Beethoven's Ninth Symphony which was televised live across the world on Christmas Day.

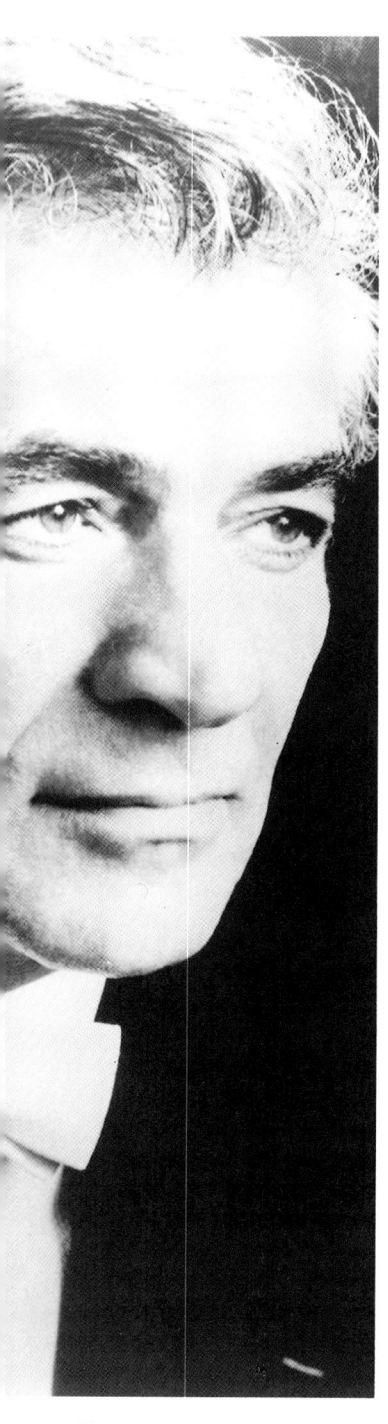

Last performance

With Leonard Bernstein's health deteriorating rapidly and due to his typical refusal to cancel engagements in order to be properly treated, Bernstein became very frail. However, he was able to attend the beginning of one of his projects – a Pacific Music Festival to be based in Japan – and provide new opportunities for music making and music appreciation.

In the summer of 1990, Bernstein conducted at Tanglewood for the last time. During a performance of Beethoven's Seventh Symphony he felt so unwell that he was barely able to continue conducting. The Boston Symphony Orchestra, from a mixture of love for Bernstein and professionalism, managed to finish the concert. It was his last performance.

Leonard Bernstein returned to New York, scene of some of his greatest triumphs, where he died on October 14, 1990 from a bronchial condition and from overextending himself in pursuit of his genius. He was aged seventy-two.

The legacy

The world of classical music was devastated by the news of his death. Leonard Bernstein was a legend. He will be remembered for his achievements as composer, conductor, performer, and educator, but best of all, for being a lovely man. Leonard Bernstein left a handful of Broadway shows that changed the direction of the American musical. His influence on conducting is best seen in the work of those who followed him and studied with him. Many of these went on to direct some of the world's great orchestras. His symphonic compositions have found a secure place in the repertoire of orchestras throughout the world.

The city of New York arranged a special concert in his memory. The orchestra consisted of players from his best-loved orchestras – New York, London, and Vienna. At the beginning, with the orchestra assembled on the stage, a door in the wings opened but nobody came through it. The orchestra played the overture to *Candide* without a conductor. It was a great tribute to the memory of an irreplaceable man.

Important Dates

1918	Aug. 25: Leonard Bernstein, officially named Louis, is born in Lawrence, Massachusetts to parents Sam and Jennie Bernstein.
1929	Leonard enters the Boston Latin School and begins piano lessons.
1932	May: Leonard attends his first classical concert, given by the Boston Symphony Orchestra, with his father.
1935	Leonard leaves the Boston Latin School and applies for a place at Harvard University to study music.
1937	Bernstein meets conductor Dimitri Mitropoulos who influences his choice of conducting as a career. Nov. 14: Bernstein meets the composer Aaron Copland, who has a great influence on Bernstein's musical style.
1939	June 22: Bernstein, aged twenty, graduates from Harvard University. Bernstein enters the Curtis Institute of Music, Philadelphia, to study conducting under the guidance of Fritz Reiner.
1940	Feb. 24: One of Bernstein's compositions is broadcast from the Institute. Bernstein attends The Boston Symphony Orchestra's summer school at Tanglewood in New Hampshire under the teaching of Serge Koussevitsky.
1941	Bernstein leaves the Curtis Institute.
1942	Bernstein moves to New York. Bernstein composes his first symphony, the *Jeremiah Symphony*.
1943	Aug. 24: Artur Rodzinski appoints Bernstein as his assistant conductor of the New York Philharmonic Orchestra. Bernstein begins to work on his first ballet, *Fancy Free*, with Jerome Robbins. Nov. 14: Bernstein's debut performance as conductor of the New York Philharmonic Orchestra is well received.
1944	Jan. 28: Bernstein's first symphony, *Jeremiah*, opens in Pittsburgh. Dec. 28: Bernstein's first musical, *On the Town*, opens in New York.
1946	Feb.: Bernstein meets his future wife, Chilean actress and pianist, Felicia Montealegre Cohn. Bernstein makes his European conducting debuts in Prague and London.
1947	Bernstein is invited to conduct the Palestine Symphony Orchestra in Palestine and is received with wide acclaim.
1949	Bernstein completes his second symphony, *The Age of Anxiety*.
1951	Bernstein and Koussevitsky share the conducting for the Israel Philharmonic Orchestra's first visit to the United States. June 6: Serge Koussevitsky dies. Sept. 9: Bernstein marries Felicia Montealegre Cohn.
1952	The Bernstein's first child, Jamie, is born.
1953	Feb. 21: Bernstein's new musical, *Wonderful Town*, opens to rave reviews in New York. It runs for 559 performances.
1955	The movie *On the Waterfront*, with musical score by Bernstein, wins an Academy Award for Best Picture. Leonard Bernstein's wife, Felicia, gives birth to their son, Alexander.

1956	Bernstein's musical, *Candide*, opens in New York.
1957	Aug. 19: Bernstein's most famous musical, *West Side Story*, is performed for the first time in Washington. Following the New York première in September, it goes on to play on Broadway for a year and a half.
1958	Bernstein becames the first American-born musical director of the New York Philharmonic Orchestra. Bernstein begins a very successful series of "Young People's Concerts" on television.
1959	Bernstein takes his orchestra on a tour of the Soviet Union. Nov: Bernstein's first book, *The Joy of Music*, is published.
1960	Bernstein celebrates the centenary of Gustav Mahler's birth with a series of concerts in New York.
1961	Oct. 18: The movie of *West Side Story* is released.
1962	The Bernstein's third child, Nina, is born.
1963	Bernstein's third symphony *Kaddish* is performed in Israel.
1965	Bernstein composes *Chichester Psalms* – a religious piece for Chichester Cathedral, in Britain.
1969	April 30: Bernstein's father dies.
1971	Sept. 8: The first performance of *Mass*, subtitled "A Piece for Singers, Players and Dancers," in memory of John F. Kennedy takes place in Washington. Dec. 15: Bernstein conducts his one thousandth performance with the New York Philharmonic.
1973	Leonard conducts a series of lectures for Harvard University on the history of music called "The Unanswered Question," which is televised worldwide.
1976	Bernstein and Felicia separate, but are reconciled when it is found that Felicia has cancer.
1977	Jan 19: Bernstein conducts his last major composition *Songfest* to commemorate the inauguration of President Carter.
1978	June 16: Bernstein's wife, Felicia, dies.
1989	Dec. 25: After the collapse of the Berlin wall, Bernstein leads a performance of Beethoven's Ninth Symphony in Berlin.
1990	Oct. 14: Leonard Bernstein dies, aged seventy-two.

Glossary

Acoustics: The science of sound waves and how they are transmitted.
Anglican: Relating to the Church of England.
Anti-Semitism: Discrimination against or persecution of the Jewish race.
Ballad: A simple song, usually telling a story, with a repeating refrain.
Big Apple: New York.
Broadway: A street in New York that has become famous in the theatrical world and attracts the most successful stage shows.
Cabaret: A form of entertainment, of dancing or singing, usually in a night-club.
Catholic: A denomination of the Christian church.
Choreography: The arrangement and sequence of steps and movements in a dance.
Cold War: Hostilities that existed between the Eastern and Western worlds, in particular between the USSR and the United States, after World War II.
Composition: The act of creating a piece of work, in this instance, a musical piece.
Concerto: A musical *composition* for a solo instrument accompanied by an orchestra.
Conga: A type of dance performed in Cuba.
Grand piano: A type of piano where the strings are arranged horizontally.
Jazz: A style of music developed in the southern states of America in the early twentieth century. It is characterized by its strong rhythms and improvised melodies.
Jew: Someone who follows the Jewish or Semitic faith, which is descended from the ancient Israelites.
Laureate: A title given to a person in recognition of their outstanding skill in a particular field, such as Poet Laureate or Laureate Conductor.
Lutheran: A follower of the teachings of Martin Luther, the founder of the *Protestant* Church.
Mass: A musical setting, written in five parts of the church service, or Eucharist, in Christian worship.
Nazis: A political party with strong ideological beliefs about race and nationality which seized power in Germany in the 1930s.
Opera: A stage drama where the words are set to music and accompanied by an orchestra.
Operetta: A type of light-hearted *opera*.
Orchestration: The arrangement of a piece of music to be played by an orchestra.
Oscar: An annual award given by the U.S. Academy of Motion Picture Arts and Sciences for outstanding achievement in movie production, acting, and so on.
Protestant: A follower of any branch of the Christian faith that was separated from the Roman *Catholic* Church at the Reformation.
Puritan: Someone who follows a very pure or extreme form of the *Protestant* faith.
Repertoire: A collection of works that an artist is able to perform.
Revue: A light-hearted entertainment, which makes fun of topical events, performed on the stage.
Score: A *composition* in which the music for the instruments is written down formally on the page.
Sonata: A musical *composition* for solo piano or for a solo instrument with piano accompaniment.
Symphony: A large-scale piece of music, in several movements, for a full orchestra.
Variation: A theme that is repeated in a variety of ways throughout a piece of music.
Viennese Waltz: A ballroom dance originating from Vienna.
Virtuoso: Someone who is recognized to be a master of an artistic technique, such as music.

Recommended Listening

Bernstein's compositions: *West Side Story* – All the music from this musical is exciting and memorable. The songs, such as "Maria" and "America," have become very famous. "Tonight" is very unusual – in this song, Bernstein interweaves the thoughts of five different people. The dances are also central to the piece – the music is often fast and aggressive, with both American elements and Puerto Rican rhythms.
Symphonies 1 (*Jeremiah*) and 2 (*The Age of Anxiety*) – Early tributes to Bernstein's Jewish background and to the influence of his father is apparent in the first symphony. The second contains some of his loveliest music for piano and orchestra.
Candide – Bernstein's last major recording of his own music and the final version of his troubled, but wonderful, operetta.

Bernstein as a conductor: There are many recordings which represent Bernstein as a conductor. Of particular interest are his recordings of the works of his hero Gustav Mahler, Gershwin's *Rhapsody in Blue* and Copland's *Appalachian Spring*. Bernstein himself considered his version of Beethoven's late String Quartets played by the Vienna Philharmonic to be amongst his finest recordings.

Index

Age of Anxiety, The 43
"America" 52
Anti-Semitism 19
Arias and Barcarolles 59

Bernstein, Alexander (son) 45
Bernstein, Felicia (née Montealegre Cohn) 41, 43, 45, 53, 58
Bernstein, Jamie (daughter) 45
Bernstein, Nina (daughter) 53
Bernstein, Leonard
  and Felicia Bernstein 41, 43, 45, 53, 56
  birth of 9-10,
  books by 52, 58
  and the Boston Latin School 16, 18
  and Betty Camden 39, 46
  character of 6, 16, 19, 22, 23, 33, 53, 59
  children of 45, 53
  and Helen Coates 14, 18, 29, 42
  as composer 5, 24, 34, 40, 44, 52, 59, 60
  as conductor 6, 17, 21, 26-29, 30, 31, 33, 35-39, 40, 41, 44, 45, 52, 54, 55, 59, 60
  and Aaron Copland 23-24, 26, 30, 34
  and the Curtis Institute of Music 26, 29-30, 33
  death of 60
  early years of 11-15, 16
  the educator 6, 21-22, 52, 57-58, 60
  and Adolph Green 23, 34, 46
  health of 10-11, 32, 54, 56, 58-60
  at Harvard University 18-20, 24-25, 26, 57
  and Jewish faith 19, 32, 33, 34, 35, 54-55
  and Serge Koussevitzky 30, 31, 32, 34, 35, 38, 40, 43, 44, 45
  marriage of 45, 58
  and Dimitri Mitropoulos 20-21, 25-26, 30
  musical compositions of 5, 6, 34-35, 39, 40, 41, 43, 46, 47, 48-52, 55, 57, 58, 59, 60
  musical influences on 6, 12, 13, 14, 15, 17, 20, 23, 24, 34, 40, 44, 48
  musical style of 12-13
  and the New England Conservatory 12, 34
  and New York 25, 34, 40-41, 46, 60
  and orchestras 7, 20, 30, 35-38, 40, 43, 44, 52, 53, 55-56, 60
  as pianist 6, 11, 24, 25, 32, 34, 40, 60
  relationship with father 10-13, 17-18, 35, 37, 42, 56
  relationship with mother 10, 18, 20
  and Jerome Robbins 39, 40, 46, 49
  at Tanglewood 30-31, 60
  and sexuality 21, 25, 41, 53, 58
  and the United States of America 6, 7-8, 32-33, 39, 43, 52
Bernstein, Jennie (née Reswick, mother) 9, 10, 18, 20
Bernstein, Sam (father) 8-9, 10, 11, 12, 13, 17, 18, 35, 37, 42, 56-57
Boston Latin School 16, 18
Boston Symphony Orchestra 20, 30, 43, 60

Camden, Betty 39, 46
Candide, 6, 47, 48, 60
Chichester Psalms 55
Coates, Helen 14, 18, 29, 42
Copland, Aaron 23-24, 26, 30, 34
Conducting, the art of 27-29
Curtis Institute of Music, The 26, 29-30, 33

Facsimile 41
Fancy Free 39

Gershwin, George 16, 22
Gilbert and Sullivan 16, 22-23, 48
"Glitter and be Gay" 48
Green, Adolph 23, 25, 34, 46

Harvard University 18-20, 24-25, 26, 57
Hitler, Adolf 31, 32, 34, 55
"I Hate Music" 37
Israel Philharmonic Orchestra 44

Jazz 15-16, 23, 34, 40, 44, 57, **63**
Jeremiah Symphony 34-35, 43, 57
Joy of Music, The 52

Kaddish 54, 57
Koussevitzky, Serge 30, 31, 32, 34, 35, 38, 40, 43, 44, 45

"A Little Bit in Love" 47
London Philharmonic Orchestra 40

Mahler, Gustav 44, 54, 55
Mass: "A Piece for Singers, Players, and Dancers" 57
Mitropoulos, Dimitri 20-21, 25-26, 30

New England Conservatory of Music 12, 34
"New York, New York" 40
New York Philharmonic Orchestra 7, 35, 37-38, 52, 53, 54, 56, 57

On the Town 6, 39, 40, 46
On the Waterfront 47

Palestine Symphony Orchestra 43
Piano Variations 23, 24
Prokofiev, Serge 14

Robbins, Jerome 39, 40, 46, 49

"Somewhere" 52
Sonata for Clarinet and Piano 34
Songfest 58
Stravinsky, Igor 14, 23, 34

Tanglewood 30-31, 60
"Tonight" 52

Unanswered Question, The 58
Vienna Philharmonic Orchestra 55-56
West Side Story 5, 48-52, 55
  songs from 52
Wonderful Town 46-47
World War II 8, 32, 33, 34, 42, 43
  persecution of the Jews 8, 32, 34-35